Keeper of Soles

by

TERESA BATEMAN

illustrated by YAYO

Holiday House / New York

For Janeen and Amy, who also have
quick wits and kind hearts
T. B.

To my flat feet
Y.

Text copyright © 2006 by Teresa Bateman
Illustrations copyright © 2006 by Diego Herrera (Yayo)
All Rights Reserved
Printed in the United States of America
The artwork was created in acrylics on Arches watercolor paper.
The text typeface is Fritz Book.
www.holidayhouse.com
3 5 7 9 10 8 6 4 2

Library of Congress Cataloging-in-Publication Data

Bateman, Teresa.
Keeper of soles / by Teresa Bateman ; illustrated by Yayo.—1st ed.
p. cm.
Summary: A shoemaker repeatedly outwits a black-robed figure
who knocks on the shoemaker's door and demands his soul.
ISBN 0-8234-1734-4
[1. Shoemakers—Fiction. 2. Shoes—Fiction. 3. Death—Fiction.]
I. Yayo, ill. II. Title.
PZ7+
[E]—dc22
2004052297

ISBN-13: 978-0-8234-1734-6 (hardcover)
ISBN-13: 978-0-8234-2137-4 (paperback)

Colin was the best shoemaker in the kingdom. He made shoes for dancers that were as light as air, walking shoes that promised nary a blister, baby shoes that made children wish to walk, and ladies' shoes that made any woman who wore them beautiful.

There was magic in Colin's cobbling, people said. Colin just laughed.

"A well-made shoe does what it's supposed to do," he said.

People came from far and near to buy Colin's shoes. He could have easily made a fortune. Indeed, some of his shoes sold for great amounts—those with gold or ruby insets, for example. But the profit Colin made on rich people's shoes was offset by the profit he lost on the shoes he made for the less fortunate. Those he sold for mere coppers, though the workmanship was just as fine as the others, if the materials were not quite so grand.

As the years passed, more and more people came to depend on the cobbler. Then, one night, a knock came at his door—a slow, thudding sound—and a cold wind slithered in. Colin moved closer to the fire, sure he imagined the knock.

It came again, and he could deny it no longer. With a strange sort of dread, Colin swung open the door to find a tall figure cloaked in black filling the doorway.

The figure stepped inside and pulled a parchment from a long, dark sleeve.

"I'm Death," he declared in a voice that spoke of graveyards and dark, starless nights. "Are you Colin the cobbler?"

For a moment Colin was tempted to say that he wasn't, but, being a truthful man, he nodded his head.

"I am. What do you wish?"

"What does Death ever wish?" his dark visitor replied. "I've come for your soul. Your time has passed and you must go with me."

Colin looked at the work left undone on his bench, and he thought of the feet that would go cold and bare. Then he took a closer look at Death.

"You're barefoot!" he blurted.

Death seemed startled. Most people, when facing that solemn journey to the other side, did not comment on feet. He raised his black robe slightly.

"What of it?" Death asked.

An idea crossed Colin's mind. "Have you ever noticed," he said casually, "that your feet hurt after work?"

"After work?" Death asked, as if such a concept was foreign to him, which, Colin supposed, it was.

"What you need is a good pair of shoes," Colin continued.

Death was used to people trying to bargain their way out of his services. Nobody before, however, had inquired after his footwear. He scanned the parchment again to get back into his normal routine. "Ah, here you are," he said in a deep and mournful voice.

"Yes, definitely shoes," Colin continued. "Could I borrow that for a moment?"

He snatched Death's parchment out of his hand and placed it on the floor. "Just step here and I'll make a pattern."

Bemused, Death did as he was told. Colin grabbed a piece of charcoal and sketched around Death's feet. Then, blowing on his hands, for they were now deathly cold, he cut out the pattern.

"Sandals, I think," Colin said, considering. "They would go with the robe."

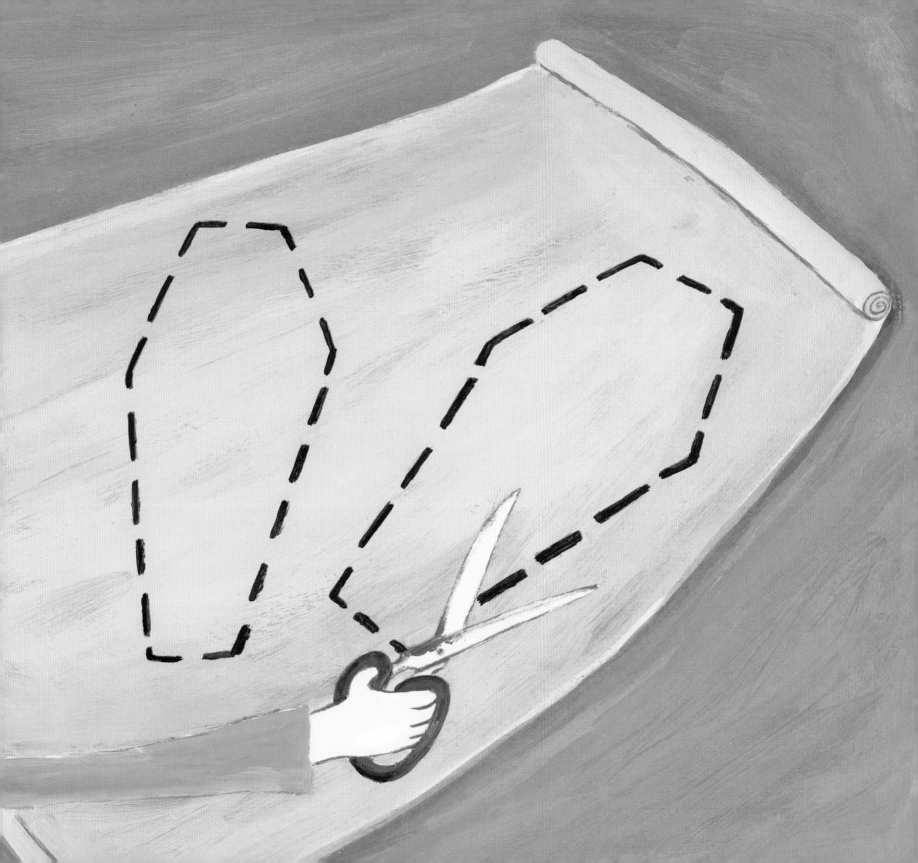

By now Death was thoroughly confused. He stood silently as Colin sketched a quick design for his sandals and promised him they would be ready in a month.

"Well, if that's all," Colin concluded, "I'll see you in four weeks."

He ushered Death out the door, closing it swiftly behind him.

For a moment Colin waited, fearing to hear that knock again, but Death must have been completely flustered, for he did not come back that night.

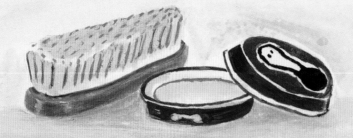

Four weeks later, however, Colin was heading to bed when he heard that same slow knock again.

Reluctantly, he swung open the door, and Death stood on the doorstep with a new parchment.

"You are Colin the cobbler?" he asked. "I have come for—"

"For your sandals, of course," Colin interrupted. "They're ready and waiting for you. I think you'll be pleased. Here, have a seat."

He pulled out his cobbler's stool and sat Death down on it.

"Lift up your feet and let me try these on you."

Colin knelt before Death and eased the new sandals over his bare toes. The chill on the floor was awful, but Colin buckled on the sandals firmly, then stood.

"Now, try them out," he urged.

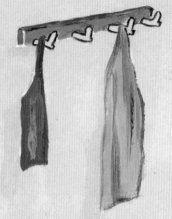

Death rose with a wrathful expression, then glanced down in wonder. The sandals were very comfortable. He had never worn shoes of any kind before. He walked around the room, for once not feeling the floor through the leathery soles of his feet.

Death hardly noticed when Colin opened the door as he made his third pass around the room and gently urged him out.

"Try those out for a week or two and let me know how you like them," the cobbler said, before closing the door firmly at Death's back.

Death must have taken his advice, for he did not return that night.

It was two weeks later that a familiar knock came to Colin's door. Sure enough, Death was waiting for him again.

"I've come—," Death began.

"I'm so glad," Colin replied. "So, how are the sandals?"

Death looked down. "They are very nice. I hadn't realized how much my feet hurt until I got them."

"I'm delighted," Colin said. "But I've been thinking. You go all over the world. Doubtless there are places where it's quite cold. You really need a sturdy pair of boots for bad weather."

"What I need—," Death began again, but Colin hurried on.

"The boots will take only a few weeks," he said. "Do you prefer brown leather or black? Yes, of course, black. Something that will blend in nicely with the robe.

"I'll have those ready by the middle of next month," he continued, ushering Death out.

He shut the door and held his breath. No knock.

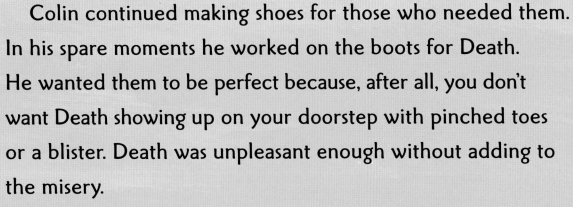

Colin continued making shoes for those who needed them. In his spare moments he worked on the boots for Death. He wanted them to be perfect because, after all, you don't want Death showing up on your doorstep with pinched toes or a blister. Death was unpleasant enough without adding to the misery.

The boots were finished and found a place at the top of a cabinet. Many customers wanted to buy them, but Colin refused each offer.

"Sorry, those are for a special client," he would always reply.

When the middle of the next month arrived, Death knocked on Colin's door. By now this had become routine. Colin removed Death's sandals and placed the boots in their stead. He could tell Death found them comfortable. It was at this point Colin suggested that perhaps Death might want something a little sportier.

"Boots are fine for bad weather, but you must cover a lot of ground. A good walking shoe with a solid tread and arch supports would be perfect."

Another month until the new pair would be done, and Death was out the door again, boots on his feet and sandals in his hand.

The walking shoes were followed by soft slippers, then fancy court shoes for special occasions. This went on for years. Colin grew older, and Death visited him often enough that they became friends, if such can be said of Death.

Finally, Colin knew he had made every type of shoe imaginable. What would he do when Death knocked again?

As always, the knock came on the door in the late night. When Death entered, he pulled out the parchment without pause.

"I have come for your soul," Death intoned, "and I will not be denied this time."

Colin smiled.

"And what do you think I've been giving you all these many years?" he asked Death. "I've given you sole after sole."

There was a dark and ominous silence. Colin could not look at Death, so he stared down at the warm and comfortable shoes that Death wore.

Then a strange sound broke the silence, a sound Colin had hardly dared believe he would hear. Death was laughing!

"Cobbler," Death said, "you speak the truth, and I cannot deny it. All men must come with me eventually, but I'll wait until the soles you have given me have worn out. Then I'll come for the soul I should have taken in the first place."

Colin smiled. Death would wear out his shoes eventually, but they were good shoes, solid shoes, well-made shoes. It would be many years before Death would stand on his doorstep again.